OMA:
A Heroine of the Holocaust

Cynthia Herschkowitch

OMA: A Heroine of the Holocaust

© Cynthia Herschkowitch, 2014

Book and cover design by Jeanne Ann Macejko

ISBN (sc) 978-1512048193

For additional information contact
Cynthia Herschkowitch
hersch48@peoplepc.com

Acknowledgements

While several people were instrumental in helping me complete this project, I first have to thank Johanna van Dam Herschkowitsch, who gave me the inspiration and the information I needed to tell her amazing story. Not only did she want me to record her oral history, she provided me with family documents, letters, pictures and personal accounts. After my newspaper article about her appeared in the *Dallas Morning News*, additional people contributed photos and information vital to the story.

In addition, I have to thank the Farmers Branch Writers Organization for encouraging me and critiquing my work, especially Jeanne Macejko who provided invaluable technical support.

To my co-writer and contributor—my daughter Delia—I offer my eternal gratitude for your input and your technical assistance. I know it has been difficult for you to re-live so many of these stories through the eyes of your beloved Oma.

A special thank-you goes to my very patient family, especially my mom, Betty Deaton, and my sister, Deborah Luttrell, for their encouragement and support in this endeavor. They loved Oma, too, and know how important it is for me to get her story out there.

To my former student and dear friend Gerardo Ramos—the valedictorian of South Oak Cliff High School's Class of 2010 and graduate of the University of Texas' Class of 2015 School of Mechanical Engineering—many thanks for your advice and technical expertise! Thanks for compiling everything and making it look so easy!

10B Sunday, December 6, 2009   dallasnews.com   The Dallas Morning News

Community opinions A forum for readers in Dallas County

A real heroine of her time

My relative risked all during the Holocaust, says **Cynthia Herschkowitsch**

Last August, a great lady and a true heroine of the Holocaust passed away quietly after a brief illness in Dallas. Although she didn't want an obituary or a funeral, her family had the briefest of obituaries published and held a remembrance gathering at her home for her close friends and family.

Johanna Herschkowitsch, my mother-in-law, was born in Hoorn, Holland, on May 7, 1919. Her father was a renowned chemist who was instrumental in early research on pasteurization. She also studied to be a chemist, but World War II changed her plans.

Voices
Teacher

With the outbreak of the war and the occupation of Holland, Johanna and her family were soon active in the Dutch Underground. These valiant people risked their lives to help the victims of the Nazi persecution by smuggling rationing coupons to buy extra food and cigarettes for people in hiding, along with letters from loved ones. Johanna had a big coat with hidden pockets that she filled with these forbidden items as she rode her bicycle from one village to another.

She often told me stories about her experiences in the war, and I persuaded her to allow me to videotape her recounting some of them. The story that always brought tears to my eyes was about her husband, Wolfgang.

As a Jew, he had left Germany to seek sanctuary in The Hague. He worked there for a while in a bookstore but inevitably got his "call-up" notice to report to a detention center. Instead, he went to the small village of Driebergen where he put an ad in the local gazette seeking to join a quartet. Johanna and two of her friends, the Akkerman brothers, had a trio, and they responded to his ad, and they began playing together.

Sometime later, Wolfgang disappeared. Johanna had no idea where he was and knew better than to ask questions. In the meantime, she got into a scrape with the Nazis when all college students were required to sign an oath of allegiance to Germany, and she refused. Instead of reporting to a detention center as ordered, she got on her bike and rode to a little farming village about 70 miles away and hid out for several months.

A year after Wolfgang disappeared, she got an invitation to have dinner at the Akkermans' house. After dinner, Anton said, "I have a surprise for you," and whistled a few bars from Mozart's "Hunt Quartet." A door to the attic opened, and Wolfgang emerged from his

hiding place to a joyous reunion. He spent two years in hiding until the Dutch Liberation in 1945, which, coincidentally, occurred on Johanna's birthday, May 7.

After the war, Johanna and Wolfgang married and emigrated to the United States. Although he had a degree in jurisprudence from a German university, he couldn't practice law here. Instead, he turned to music. He and Johanna made beautiful music together for many years playing with the Dallas Symphony Orchestra — he, as a violinist; she, as a cellist. They became U.S. citizens, voted religiously and participated in the American Dream.

She was a very firm believer in the power of education and expected all of us to take advantage of the many opportunities available to us in this free country. She helped put me and her grandchildren through school. I only recently learned that she also helped pay for the education of the daughter of Anton Akkerman, who had hidden Wolfgang during the war.

She didn't want a memorial, but she left a living legacy — the gift of knowledge.

Cynthia Herschkowitsch teaches at South Oak Cliff High School in Dallas ISD and is a Teacher Voices volunteer columnist. Her e-mail address is CHerschkowitsch@dallasisd.org.

DALLAS MORNING NEWS ARTICLE
by Cynthia Herschkowitsch

In August of 2008, a great lady and a true heroine of the Holocaust passed away quietly after a brief illness in Dallas. Although she didn't want an obituary or a funeral, her family had the briefest of obituaries published and held a remembrance gathering at her home for her close friends and family.

Johanna Herschkowitsch, nee van Dam, was born in Hoorn, Holland, on May 7, 1919. Her father was a renowned chemist who was instrumental in early research on pasteurization. She also studied to be a chemist, but World War II changed her plans. With the outbreak of the war and the occupation of Holland, Johanna and her family were soon active in the Dutch Underground. These valiant people risked their lives to help the victims of the Nazi persecution by smuggling rationing coupons to buy extra food and cigarettes for people in hiding, along with letters from loved ones. Johanna had a big coat with hidden pockets that she filled with these forbidden items as she rode her bicycle from one village to another. More than once, she was stopped and interrogated. One time, however, she got the scare of her life when, laden with contraband, a soldier detained her and was going to arrest her because she wore a daisy on her coat. The daisy was the symbol of Princess Margarethe of the Dutch Royal Family who were popular because of their opposition to the Nazis. Realizing that she had put not only herself but the others who depended on her in jeopardy, she never made that mistake again.

She often told me stories about her experiences in the war, and I suggested that she should participate in Steven Spielberg's video archives of Holocaust survivors, but she declined, saying she was "too old and her memories too vague." Fearing I would forget the details of her saga, I persuaded her to allow me to videotape her recounting some of them. One time, she told me, her cousin Jan, who had a penchant for being absent-minded and chronically late, showed up at a meeting of the Underground three hours late to tell them he couldn't attend the 8:00 meeting. But the story that always brought tears to my eyes was about her husband Wolfgang. As a Jew, he had left Germany to seek sanctuary in The Hague. He worked there for a while in a bookstore but inevitably got his "call-up" notice to report to a detention center. (The Nazis cleverly avoided mentioning that he would be put on the slow train but fast track to a concentration camp if he reported.) Instead, he went to the small village of Driebergen where he put an ad in the local gazette seeking to join a quartet. As Johanna and two of her friends, the Akkerman brothers, had a trio, they responded to this would-be fourth member with "the funny name" and began playing together. Some time later, Wolfgang disappeared. Johanna had no idea where he was and knew better than to ask questions. In the meantime, she got into another scrape with the Nazis when all college students were required to sign an oath of allegiance to Germany and she refused. Instead of reporting to a detention center as ordered, she got on her bike and rode to a little farming village about seventy miles away and hid out for several months. A year after Wolfgang disappeared,she got an invitation to have dinner at the Akkerman's house. After dinner, Anton said, "I have a surprise for you," and whistled a few bars from Mozart's "Hunt Quartet." A door to the attic opened, and Wolfgang emerged from his hiding place to a joyous reunion. He eventually spent three years in hiding until the Dutch Liberation which, coincidentally, occurred on Johanna's birthday, May 7, 1945.

After the war, Johanna and Wolfgang married and emigrated to the United States. Although he had a degree in jurisprudence from a German university, he couldn't practice law here. Instead, he turned to music. He and Johanna made beautiful music together for many years playing with the Dallas Symphony Orchestra—he, as a violinist; she, as a cellist. They became U.S. citizens, voted religiously and participated in the American Dream. After Wolfgang died in 1971, Johanna continued to play for a while but retired when she turned sixty-five. Not one to stay idle, she traveled and took Spanish lessons. She was a very firm believer in the power of education and expected all of us to take advantage of the many opportunities available to us in this free country. She not only helped finance her son's education, she helped with my education, her two granddaughters, and, I only recently learned, with the education of the daughter of Anton Akkerman, who had hidden Wolfgang during the war. She didn't want a memorial, but she left a living legacy—the gift of knowledge.

CHAPTER ONE
THE MOTIVATION

"Mom, the universe is talking to you," my daughter recently observed during a phone conversation.

"Yes, I know," I replied, somewhat dispiritedly. "But I was hoping to wait until I retire to start such an ambitious project."

Now, however, it seemed imperative for me to get started without further delay.

Even before my mother-in-law passed away in 2008, I had planned to write a book detailing her family tales and her experiences as a member of the Dutch Underground in World War II. And how she met and married her husband, a Holocaust survivor. Such a romantic story, it always makes me cry.

But I'm getting ahead of myself. The beginning was inauspicious enough. After I graduated from high school, I dutifully went to college without a goal in mind. I was lost and lacked focus. So when I met my husband-to-be, my objective was suddenly clarified: I'll get married, and life will work itself out! What I had no way of knowing is that my ill-considered decision would catapult me from my sheltered, small-town, myopic lifestyle into a life-affirming, viewpoint-broadening way of life that was international in scope. Sadly, the marriage lasted only five years, but my relationship with my mother-in-law endured for over forty years, and her impact on my life is immeasurable.

My former husband's parents were not at all happy about our marriage. We were too young, too stupid, too poor—we had nothing to cement a relationship. But you know, kids never listen. At first, they contacted a lawyer, hoping to get the marriage annulled, but the lawyer found that the marriage was binding. Although they gave up on that idea, they still weren't happy, and they didn't warm up to me until our daughter was born two years later and, then, only grudgingly. By that time, Wolfgang was in a fight for his life for, despite having endured the Holocaust, he—like many of his generation—was a heavy smoker—unfiltered Camels. He and Johanna tried conventional and alternative therapies. They traveled to Mexico for laetrile injections. Supposedly, the almond extract had cancer-fighting properties. But it didn't work. He suffered terribly that last year of his life, but I think he had some solace from the fact that I had returned to North Texas State University to become a teacher, majoring in English, minoring in German. He also doted on—and delighted in—my daughter, his only grandchild, Delia. Many years later, at the memorial gathering we held after Johanna's death, I was told by a neighbor who was just a boy at the time, that Wolfgang had once remarked to him: "I thought the marriage was a mistake. They were too young. But that little girl has brought me so much joy!"

Despite the break-up of our marriage and for Delia's sake, I continued visiting Johanna. Frequently during the summers, I would take Delia and we would meet Johanna in Holland, her birthplace, where she would relentlessly take us to various places of personal and historical significance. Her knowledge of Holland's history was voluminous, and she was determined to transmit it all to me—I guess so that I could, in turn, pass it on to Delia as she grew older and more capable of absorbing it. We rode bikes, trains and "bromfiets," and saw many museums—oh, so many museums—and Madurodam, Sneek, Volendam, Marken, Gouda, Scheveningen, Amsterdam (one of my favorite places on earth and not for the same reason that many people like it) and, of course, her hometown, Hoorn. I've watched elderly Dutch ladies tat; I've watched poffertjes being cooked; I've braved the peanut sauce of the Rijstafel and seen a Grand Prix race in the sand dunes of Zaandvoort. At the height of the hippie era, I saw "Hair" performed in A'dam; I've seen the workings of virtually every type of windmill ever created. I've been to the Zuider Zee, seen polders and new towns built on land reclaimed from an inexorable sea. And through all of the visits and the tours, I listened to the stories—stories about the family, the war, the "Hunger Winter," the deprivation, the search for potatoes in the dark, the Liberation, the aftermath of the war, the relocation to the United States, the new life born of the Holocaust. And I always thought, "This story needs to be told."

After Wolf died in 1971, Johanna continued to play cello in the Dallas Symphony Orchestra, but she retired in 1984. As she got older, I began to worry that the stories would be lost. When "Schindler's List" came out, Steven Spielberg began looking for Holocaust survivors to tell their stories and set up his Shoah Foundation as a clearinghouse for oral histories. I contacted the foundation to ask them about Johanna and what her oral history would entail. There were forms to complete and, if her story was accepted, she would be interviewed by someone from the foundation. She would not agree to that; however, she was perfectly willing for me to videotape her as she recounted her experiences. Great. I had never even used a video camera and felt ill-prepared to do the project. But I felt strongly that it should be done. So on several occasions, I went to her house—sometimes with Delia; sometimes, alone—as she endeavored to document the events of her life. She always came prepared; she made an outline or list of things she wanted to cover in each session. At its completion, I had about four hours of her on videotape, and I am eternally grateful that I do, for there is absolutely no way that I could ever have recalled the many details of her life. And because she was so forthcoming in her discourse, I believe that she knew how important some of the events were in the grand scheme of things and wanted her story to be told and shared and not lost to the vagaries of time. And that's why I began to feel the pressure of the universe in providing the venue for her story to be told.

CHAPTER TWO
THE VAN DAM FAMILY

Hoorn is a beautiful old fishing village nestled along the northwestern part of the Netherlands in the Ijsselmeer, an area reclaimed from the sea by very determined Dutch engineers. Some would call it "quaint," but that is giving it a connotation undeserved in light of its harsh climate and Spartan way of life. The people who live there are sturdy and stoic; the harbor is still filled with full-masted sailing ships which require strength and stamina to maintain in the back-breaking work of fishing for eels. The sea is an unforgiving place, and the people who live near the sea or have to make their living from the sea have to be resolute and resilient. The Dutch realized early on that, if they were going to have any chance of expanding their small country, they were going to have to create new land. Not for nothing is Holland designated one of the "low countries." It is several feet below sea level. The fact that there is an Amsterdam at all is based solely on the ingenuity of the engineers who designed a plan to drive five million wooden piles into the soft soil to create a foundation for building. My hat's off to the Dutch for having the strength, courage and intelligence to tame the sea by building a series of dikes to close off polders which were then drained of water to become part of the land mass. A map of Holland in the thirteenth century shows a thin strip of land with several small islands along its coast. Now, all of the area in between has been filled in or "reclaimed." It's still a small country, but it's a country to be reckoned with; after all, the World Court is located in den Haag (the Hague).

The Dutch people as a whole are known to be

thrifty to the point of being parsimonious and conservative with their resources, although their politics are a different matter. They have always been open-minded and liberal when it comes to religion and oppressed people, opening their hearts and homes to many people seeking religious tolerance. When it comes to sex and drugs, their tolerance is legendary. After all, *High Times Magazine* holds its annual marijuana conference there every year, and the Bulldog Cafes are known to high school and college students everywhere. The Red Light District—the Zeedijk—with its "happy hookers" originated to meet the needs and desires of sailors seeking respite from sea life and comfort in the arms of the willing women. Now it is carefully regulated by the government, and the girls have to be licensed and certified. The hookers and the hashish may account for a good part of Amsterdam's tourist trade.

Among the many prominent families in Hoorn is the van Dam family, the roots of which we can trace back to the seventeenth century, thanks to an uncle who, years ago, documented the family lineage for posterity.

Johanna's mother, Nellie Cristina Maalsteed, was born in 1891 in den Helden into a family of merchant marines. As far back as we can trace the family, they were always seafarers, except her father. Because of a basic "weakness in his lungs," he was considered unfit for the merchant marines and, instead, established a dry-goods store that supplied the ships and the sailors. That he was able to continue in the family tradition, serving in some capacity to the seamen, is a testament to his Dutch heritage. As a whole, Dutch people don't give up; they persevere. Photos of Nellie's family show an austere group, wearing what would today be called "costumes" by people who have been to Marken or Volendam and seen the residents in the garb they don for tourists. But this was their everyday clothing, with aprons and white caps with ornate pins and brooches. The women, in particular, are striking, because of their stiff, expressionless faces. In showing me these photos, Johanna never failed to remark that their mask-like expression was reflective of the seasonal depression that ran rampant in her family. Nellie suffered from that depression, and while Johanna seemed free of its oppression, I suspect that her sister Alida inherited the trait, if that's what it is.

Johanna in traditional Dutch dress

1937 Fotograph

You will see the beautiful
Norwegian costumes on
some of the group-pictures
of the students.

On this dutch costume you
find the head iron with
pins, the apron and dress
etc. This is cheap metal,
but it will shine when
polished. The Sunday costume
had fancy irons and overall
nicer looking.

Johanna's note, explaining previous photo.

"Wim" and Nellie with their father,
Rudolph Maalsteed, circa 1915

Nellie's only sibling was a brother, Willem, who was born in 1895 but died on Oct. 2, 1925, barely thirty years old. Nicknamed "Wim," he was a promising musician who graduated from a music conservatory in the Hague. At the time of his death from brain cancer, he was engaged to Nellie Wagenaar, one of the daughters of the conservatory's director, Dr. Johan Wagenaar. As a tribute to his intended son-in-law, Dr. Wagenaar composed a memorial program which was performed on April 26, 1926. Wim's death hit the family hard. Afterward, they spoke his name in near-reverence, deeply regretting the loss of their only son.

"Wim" Maalsteed

Their father, Rudolph Maalsteed, ran The Old Viktualien Huis, supplying dry goods and supplies for ships. Nellie graduated from high school and went to Hoorn to study and, eventually, became certified as a pharmacist's assistant. In 1911, she got a job as a laboratory technician at the state agricultural experimental station where a man by the name of

Willem van Dam, who was eighteen years her senior, also worked. The story goes that Nellie once passed by his office and put a piece of litmus paper on his head, saying, "Oh, Mr. van Dam, I'm just trying to see if you are a sour old bachelor." They were engaged in 1912 and married in 1913, at which time she quit working to concentrate on starting a family.

Based on Johanna's account, her mother was lively and fun, cheerful and impulsive. She focused on nature, poetry, English literature and music when teaching her children and supported her husband in every endeavor. She had a club with three or four women, one of whom was an English teacher in Hoorn. In the club, Nellie read an immense amount of literature. She especially enjoyed the Romantics and quoted Keats and Shelley frequently.

Growing up, Nellie had voice training and played the piano. For her children, Nellie organized plays and musicals and made costumes with flowers and animals. She loved nature, especially "birding" and was a member of the Audubon Society. She spent hours on excursions watching gulls and the huge variety of birds on the island of Tessel. In addition to nature and literature, Nellie was a history buff and was, according to Johanna, "very nationalistic."

Johanna's father, Willem van Dam, was born in 1873 in Wageningen, a university town west of Arnhem. He was the youngest of four brothers, all of them spaced two years apart: Piet, the oldest, was a math teacher and the father of Johanna's favorite cousin, Jan; Nic was a doctor and internist at the sanitarium in Nijmegen; Jan was a high school English teacher in den Haag, and finally, there was Willem. Growing up, Willem was always good in sports. He was nimble and had great coordination and balance. He medaled in skating and played soccer and cello, which no doubt influenced Johanna in her selection of instruments. In addition to nurturing his own children, Willem's father took in students, and everyone worked hard to get good educations; that was a priority in the family. Willem got his PhD in Basel, Switzerland. From age thirty-five to sixty-five, he worked at the state agricultural experimental station, specializing in dairy. Several times, he was asked to become a professor in a university, but he preferred research. At the agricultural station, there were three branches of study: chemistry, bacteriology and physiology; he eventually became director of the chemistry department. The lab had milking machines and was very up-to-date for the time. His work began when research was in its infancy, and his research helped Holland's export business and enabled the institute to become internationally known. When Johanna was a child, she and her sister visited her father at his office on Sundays. She recalls his huge study with a large picture window. The window had a hole in it that fascinated her for some reason. Years later, after his death, she returned to his office and was amazed to discover that the hole was still there! (This is one of the things that I love about Holland. Every time I ever visited cousin Jan's house in Driebergen, I looked for the Japanese figurine on the windowsill on the stair landing. There was a tiny filament of some kind going from her outstretched hand to a corner of the window. It was always there, and I found it very comforting, as if every thing in the world might change, but that tiny corner of the world could be depended on to remain intact.) To illustrate how significant her father's research had become, on one occasion, Johanna happened to be in New York and visited Cornell University. She asked to see their research department and noticed a very familiar face in a picture hanging in

the corridors there – her father, Willem. Johanna kept
the letters that Nellie received from Cornell, thanking
her for supplying the picture. On the occasion of his
eightieth birthday, an article was published including a
list of his publications and accomplishments. Titled
"Dr. W. van Dam on his 80th birthday," the letter reads,
"On the 9th of November 1953, Dr. W. van Dam, retired
director of the chemical department of the State
Agricultural Experimental Station at Hoorn, one of the
great pioneers of scientific dairy research, celebrated
his eightieth birthday. We want to offer our
congratulations to him and to Mrs. van Dam on this
anniversary, and we wish them many happy returns of
the day. We know that we may also do this on behalf of
his friends in the Netherlands and in foreign countries.
Van Dam was one of those workers who, in the time of
empiricism, first made use of modern scientific ways of
thinking and methods of research. Nowadays we take
such things for granted, but what it meant in those
days may be demonstrated by the question, put to Prof.
van der Burg, one of van Dam's friends, by an
investigator of the old school: 'Are you already
ionized?' The results of van Dam's investigations on the
ionic concentrations in milk and dairy products, on
rennet and rennet activity, on cheese ripening, on the
crystallization of butterfat, on the process of churning,
on the consistency of butter and on the phenomena of
creaming, are well known all over the world. These
investigations have considerably influenced the
development of dairy technology. On the occasion of
this anniversary, we want to express our gratitude and
pay homage to van Dam for all his admirable work.
Signed, H. Mulder."

As anyone who has ever been to Holland knows,
the Dutch pride themselves on their array of delicious
cheeses. On my first trip there, I actually brought back

a wheel of Gouda. When I read this article, it really made me feel how significant his research had been—not in the creation of cheese, because, obviously, that had been around for centuries—but in the refinement and the improvement of different types of cheeses which are available to us today—Gouda and Edam, especially, and also in the tweaking of the aging process, which produces cheese ranging from buttery "young" flavors to strong, knock-you-down aromatic "aged" flavors that cousin Jan loved so much. Johanna recalled that the objective of one of his research projects focused on improving the aroma of butter. When Willem retired in 1938, the government bestowed on him the Distinguished Order of Oranje Nassau; he later became an officer in the Order. Johanna and her sister cherished the two medals he received—one, orange, representing the House of Oranje (the Dutch Royal Family); the other, red, white and blue. Johanna recalls her father as kind and gentle. He was, in her words, "well-liked, beautiful, innocent, and friendly with endearing blue eyes." He taught her how to ride a bicycle and how to repair things because he was "very handy." This training served her well throughout her life. In the time that I knew her, she was always quick to do repairs around the house and to build things. She loved woodworking projects and built a dining room table as well as a coffee table. Her favorite gifts were things that were made for her by hand.

Johanna's father, Willem van Dam

Because of his skating prowess, Willem taught his two daughters how to skate, and he helped them with their physics and chemistry homework. According to Johanna, he had a "great way of explaining things clearly," an ability he inherited from his own father, Jan van Dam. Recently, I ran across a statement written by Johanna about her grandfather, Jan: "My grandfather on my father's side, Jan van Dam, was born in 1841 in Stolwijk, a village southeast of Gouda. It is a quiet village with many dairy farms in the area. His wife, Teuntje Goedewaagen, was born in Gouda in 1843. Goedewaagen is a very old family, known for having made pipes and ceramics. The family is now very spread out, and there is little contact between them. Their name can be found on the bottom of modern Delft Blauw; Goedewaagen is the better brand. Jan van Dam must have been a remarkable man. He died three months after I was born in May of 1919. He was seventy-eight years old. I am sorry I have not known him. I have an article from a Wageningen newspaper, which I will condense to tell about him. In 1912 at the occasion of his retirement at age seventy, a large crowd gathered to bid farewell to the beloved director. Yes, he was always beloved; he had an indefatigable zest for his work and the respect of all. He was a self-made man with natural gifts of heart and mind. Raised in Stolwijk, he went to elementary school there until he was twelve, at which point he went to a private school in Gouda. This school also prepared students for student teaching. He was an avid learner, always wanting to absorb more knowledge. He also had his tuition paid since he soon was qualified to begin actual student teaching. In 1859 he became an assistant teacher, and a few years later, acquired certifications in math, French, English and German, all on the beginning level. He was continuously making a living in the Gouda schools. Then, from 1864 to 1866, he went to the Polytechnical Institute in Delft for subjects such as math, technology, geology, zoology, chemistry, physics, technology, and astronomy. He taught high school in Gouda until 1869 then got a teaching position at the agricultural college. In 1896, he was appointed director, a position he held until his retirement in 1912.

He helped prepare the school to become a university, which it did, a few years after he retired. There were many Indonesian students at the school. This is explained by the numerous Dutch plantations in Indonesia. To these Indonesian students, Holland was an alien environment. To them, my grandfather was a fatherly friend, always ready to help with conflicts and encouraging motivation. He had an uncanny talent for teaching and education. I found that same quality in my dad. Here I quote the article literally: 'He would talk for hours, very calmly and warm-heartedly; the fatherly expressions in his blue eyes came from the heart.' These qualities he was known for, also in the more official circles such as the Department of Education. The school became a state school in 1896. At a ceremony, he became an officer in the order of Oranje Nassau, an honor in Holland. In January of 1912, he bid the school farewell, and a large crowd assembled of colleagues, students, ex-students, and friends to pay him homage in a warm and less formal way and to tell their goodbyes and express their feelings."

The van Dam family: Nellie, Johanna, Willem and Lida.

As a teacher, I feel honored to have married into a family with such amazing educators in its history, and I am proud that my daughter, also a teacher, has a background rooted in education.

To the unlikely pair of Willem and Nellie, two children were born: Alida (or simply, Lida), the elder, a serious, no-nonsense educator; and Johanna, the younger, livelier of the two. Johanna was born on May 7, 1919—the same birthdate as Brahms and Tchaikovsky - in Hoorn. Recently, when going through some old brochures picked up while traveling years ago in Holland on several different occasions, I ran across a small book which contained a listing of major cities. Under "Hoorn," Johanna had written a note, "I was born on Graafsingel 25." It was as if she knew that I would need that information later. Johanna was named after her mother's best friend. From age three-and-a-half to five or six, she attended a Montessori school. In second grade, she began attending a public school. At eleven, she went to a high school for six years, specializing in math and science. For the last two years, she was one of only two girls in that particular school. She flourished in that environment. Naturally competitive, she very likely set out to show that "whatever a boy can do, I can do better." While there, she studied science, government, history, and "lots of languages"— French, German and three years of English. Then she went to Norway for a year to study art, weaving, home economics, and cooking, and to improve her health. While she was there, she met another student who recognized her father's name from an article about churning butter and asked her about it. It was then that she began to realize the real scope of her father's work. She graduated in 1936; she became a pharmacy technician, then a lab technician. She also studied cello. Music always played a big role in the family's life. Nellie had studied piano and had had voice training. Alida also played piano, and Willem played cello. Together, they played "Piano for Four," and they sang duets, accompanied by Lida on piano. Sometimes, they played trios with Willem on cello, Lida on piano, and Johanna on violin. Johanna, however, didn't like playing an instrument with such a high register and eventually switched to cello. This training would come in handy much later when Johanna moved to Dallas after the war and made a career out of music. This is a perfect illustration of that old maxim, "Things happen for a reason": Without her musical background, Johanna would not have had her long tenure with the Dallas Symphony Orchestra when she and Wolfgang emigrated to the United States.

The van Dam Family's sitting room. Their love of music is obvious in this photo from the 1930's.

Johanna, aged eight, practicing her sewing.

CHAPTER THREE
THE HERSCHKOWITSCH FAMILY

Wolfgang's mother, Anaeta Leviasch, was born in 1877 in Odessa , Georgia, Russia. Her father had a wholesale grain warehouse. When she was nineteen, she married Mordko Herschkowitsch who was seven or eight years older. At the time, she was studying at the piano conservatory in Leipzig and wanted to wait to get married, but Mordko told her, "We can marry, and you can still get your education." He was true to his word. After their three daughters—Rosa, Yela and Elsi—were born two years apart, Wolfgang was born seven years later. It was then that Anaeta returned to finish her studies at the conservatory. For two years, she was gone from the family from Monday through Friday. She then began giving private lessons. Mordko had been working at Zeiss-Eicon when they met and continued his work which required him to go to Brazil in 1911-1912 to find the quartz needed to make the optical lenses. He died in 1933 from an embolism in his heart during a hernia operation.

Mordko Herschkowitsch, circa 1930

The discourse which follows was dictated by Anaeta during the last year of her life to Johanna to insure that Mordko's story would be preserved for posterity. It is dated February, 1972:

"I will try to give a clear picture of Mordko through notes that have come down to me and memory. It is particularly important to know about his early years, from his tenth to eighteenth year in his development. He was born in Tusora, Russia, on February 29, 1868. His mother had died before he was ten years old; his father had remarried and they had children, so the young Mordko left his home looking for learning. A few Jewish men from the neighborhood took him with them when they went to the city. The father did not protest, and thus he came with the men in the border city Kischinew and searched there for 'the beginning of knowledge,' so to speak. The men returned, but they wanted to leave young Mordko H. in the big city. It was very difficult to find a place to stay for him; nobody wanted to take him in, but at the end of the day, a teacher was found who was willing to take in the boy. To be sure, this teacher did not have room for him either, but he had a very large table where in the daytime ten students were taught Jewish history and prayers. This table was offered young Herschkowitsch for the night, and so he spent the night sleeping on the table without pillow or blanket, and in the daytime he collected leftovers from breakfast the students had. After three days, he decided to go look around in the area and look for the school which Russia had founded after the war with Rumania. He wanted to find the director and ask him to be admitted to the school. When he came to the building, the watchman sent him on his way and told him to come back washed, combed, and buttoned. He went back three days later and did not have to pass the watchman, since the director and two teachers were standing on the grounds. They addressed the boy and were surprised about his intelligent answers, speaking in correct language, without any Rumanian accent. They also understood the boy wanted to learn; they gave him a book and a slate and showed him a place to sit, next to the wall, on the outside, and told him to pay attention what was explained to the students!

Thus, young Herschkowitsch was a student outside the school, but so to speak, went parallel to the students inside for several years until fifth grade, then two or three more years. When the time came that he was ready for graduation, nobody qualified was to be found to give the tests! He did not know what to do; he then went to a school for pharmacist's assistant studies, for which the certificate of graduation was not required. They gave their own entrance exam. He attended the school for four years, did odd jobs, tutored, and could buy the necessary books and clothing. Now military service loomed up. Because of his education, he was entitled to enlist, got an easier service and better treatment; he was even addressed with 'Sie'! (In German, it is an indication of respect, rather than the more familiar 'du.') When young Herschkowitsch came out of military service, he had no money and no clothes. He found work in a pharmacy and saved some money and tried to be admitted to the university. He was turned down and discouraged. He spoke about it to a gentleman while on his way out in the courtyard, but the man could not help him, 'The Russian Regime being very strict,' but he referred him to a colleague in Dorpath. The man Mordko H. had spoken to in the courtyard turned out to be Prof. Mendelejew, a 'star' in chemistry in Russia, and the colleague in Dorpath was Prof. Ostwald who took him under his wings. Prof. Ostwald recognized Mordko's talent and watched over him until he completed his education.

Two years passed with the preparations for admission to the University. Then followed regular study in chemistry and some special subjects for Prof. Ostwald, who kept him during the four years of the chemistry curriculum, altogether six years until the doctorate. He was allowed to write the dissertation with the guidance of two scientists, one a German physicist, and the other, a Swedish mathematician. The completion of the dissertation and the publication took another two years. And now, twenty-six years old, he was ready for a suitable job. There was an inquiry from the laboratories of Carl Zeiss and Schott Glaswerke. They needed a graduate, and Prof. Ostwald recommended him for the job. In his first year already, he worked out many new problems. He was offered to stay with a raise of M.l000.—and the prospect of a permanent position. It was for my husband very tempting, because he had had so many years of strenuous work behind him. I was his bride at the time, and ready to be married, and make M. Herschkowitsch a comfortable home. And so the years from 1899-1910 went by. At that time, Mordko heard about a Danish ship, the *Botnia*, that would make a voyage to Reykjavik. He contacted the company and was able to obtain accommodations for the passage. It was arranged with the Mayor of Reykjavik that M. Herschkowitsch would be allowed to buy rock crystal (a form of quartz). He dragged the blocks that were half-immersed in water while the donkeys were walking across them! He came home very successful and was feted.

Soon he found out that a new German ship would be launched for a long voyage. M. Herschkowitsch started discussions with the directors of Zeiss and Schott, then the government had to approve, and the captain of the ship approved the depositions. There is a picture where he boards the ship to start a world-journey. He rightaway made a plan how to use the time in the best way. First, he started to learn Spanish and did very well, to the point that he could communicate with the people ('das Volk'). He tried to pinpoint geologically where the rock-crystal was formed and was present, then by making certain deductions, find a site from which the quartz could be mined. The first pieces he packed and dispatched himself. When the time came for his return, he left two workers in charge to do the mining. It was a joyful homecoming from his successful journey. But a change had taken place. Talk of war was in the air. The ship had been declared 'war-material,' and the crew 'laborers.' Mordko had to hide in order not to be suspected of espionage. "

At this point, due to her advanced age (ninety-five), Anaeta's story (which Johanna translated from German into English) became "confused and rambling." Johanna notes that her translation of Mama's memoirs "follows her writings rather close, since I tried to retain the style of her writing." We have also been told that, after his travel to Brazil to find the "Bergkristalle," which was important for making optical instruments, he returned safely, and was greatly acknowledged and appreciated. He never interrupted his work, and he continued working for the Firma Carl Zeiss until his death in 1932. The war years (1914-1918) and inflation were never hard or filled with problems as to living conditions for him and his family. He always had a good salary and, in this respect, the family was spared the many hardships that so many people in Germany had to suffer. And he also was spared the rising tide of the Nazis. Until his death in

1932, he never took the threatening movement seriously, and he was always full of hope that something might happen to bring the movement to a halt.

In Anaeta's discourse about Mordko's life, she mentioned that Prof. Ostwald had taken young Mordko under his wing and mentored him as he continued his education. That name jogged some vague reference in my memory. Prior to working on this section, I had been reading a biography of Albert Einstein that Johanna had given me from Wolf's personal library. I recalled that, in 1901, Prof. Wilhelm Ostwald had ignored young Einstein's application to work in his laboratory. When Einstein's father followed up on the request, Prof. Ostwald also chose not to respond. I wondered if this could be the same Ostwald mentioned in connection with Mordko. Further investigation indicated that the time frame was correct, so I continued to search. Eventually, I discovered a list of "Mitarbeiter" (co-workers or colleagues) of Prof. Wilhelm Ostwald; on the list: Mordko Herschkowitsch! I found it interesting that the man who had rejected Einstein is the same man who mentored young Mordko! Ostwald must have seen something special in this young man who had come from literally nothing to be noticed by one of the greatest scientists of his time. Ostwald went on to win the Nobel Prize in Chemistry in 1909.

Recently, I received some enlightening information from an associate of Zeiss-Eicon, who informed me that "in 1903, Mordko submitted an application to become a German citizen. It was, at first, rejected. It was only approved after he contacted the Foundation commissioner at the Ministry of State in Weimar in November 1908. This shows that immigrant Jews from Russia faced considerable discrimination

also before World War I, even if they were outstanding
scientists."

The Zeiss-Eicon associate also notes that
"Mordko Herschkowitsch died on 9 June 1932. His
widow received a widow's pension from the Carl Zeiss
Foundation that was, without any reason given as
usual, raised from forty to sixty percent of the pension
along with a supplement of twelve percent. In
December 1938, she decided to leave Germany for
Holland. She asked Zeiss management to dissolve her
pension in exchange for a lump sum payment in the
amount of one year's pension in order to cover the
required securities. Management approved three times
this amount. According to the pension statutes, the
double rate was intended as a one-off payment one
year after moving abroad. This one year was included
directly in the payment. However, the Holland plans fell
through and Mrs. Herschkowitsch found a sponsor for
the USA. She received advances on the settlement
although the pension payments were not supposed to
end until the month of her departure. This enabled her
to finance her journey and pay the constantly
increasing taxes. The passage that she had already
booked in August 1939 was impossible due to the
political situation. At the last minute, she was able to
travel to the USA via Russia and Japan in August 1940.
Correspondence with Mrs. Herschkowitsch left a rather
factual impression. Unfounded special payments were
rejected, but a reason was usually found for the
financial support. Special payments and special
allowances were not questioned although the Ministry
of Education explicitly stated that benefits to Jews
could be reduced. With a monthly pension of around
three hundred-fifty marks, she received almost double
that of a worker household at the time. Even after the
settlement was paid, she received pension payments

retroactive to August 1940 minus interest for the settlement. This enabled her to pay a tax demand raised at the last minute by the tax office that threatened her departure. The reasoning that this was now possible 'because the termination of the transition period up to her departure is definite' was obviously invented."

The Herschkowitsch Family celebrating Wolf's graduation from law school: Anaeta, second from left, and Wolfgang, far right.

Did I say that the Universe was talking to me? It is now shouting at me, being very insistent! While researching this section, on April 23, 2012, I received an e-mail, out of the blue, from a gentleman in Seattle, who had just read my *Dallas Morning News* tribute to Johanna after her death in 2008. After three-and-a-half years, this man contacted me because he wrote a book , published in 2005, in which he relates information about the Herschkowitsch family. He also informs me that there is a historian in Jena (Wolfgang's birthplace) who is interested in the Herschkowitsch family! He provides me with a photo, never before seen by my daughter or me, of Elsi, the sister who died in the

Holocaust, and her baby Evelijn. Elsi looks very happy in the photo, and it makes me sad to know that she has no idea of what is to come. There are times when I start projects, and it seems as though all sorts of roadblocks and obstacles are in my path; in this case, it seems like God is blasting the obstacles out of the way and clearing the road for me to get this done.

Elsi and Evelyn (Evi) Danziger

To make it even more interesting, when I received this e-mail, it was the day before what would have been Wolf's one hundred-and-first birthday, and Delia had already planned to visit his burial site. The cemetery is large and in the middle of an urban area. While it is near Delia's home, she had not visited since she was a child, but now, she felt compelled to visit and take flowers for both her grandfather's and her great-grandmother's graves. When she got to the cemetery, she went to the office to inquire about the location of the two graves. A very tall, slender, regal gentleman offered to escort her there because the layout is so complex. When they arrived, they found a fox sitting on Wolfgang's grave! The funereal gentleman remarked, "That is very odd. Usually, he does not come out during the day. I have seen him many times around dusk, however, over by the gardeners' shed." For Delia, who is very spiritual, the fox was a sign from her grandfather that he was at peace and very touched by her visit.

Wolfgang, the darling youngest child and only son, was born on April 24, 1911 in Jena, Germany, sixty miles southwest of Leipzig. His early life was filled with books, music and nature; his father owned a lot around the corner from their home which he used as an orchard. Because of his mother's life-long devotion to musical training, music was a big part of Wolf's life. It would sustain him, years later, when he was in hiding during the war. As a child, he was introverted and sensitive, possibly a result of his older sisters' dominating personalities. When stressed, Wolf would lose himself in the comfort of his violin. While he got his sensitive side from his mother, he inherited an intensity and ability to focus from his father, which laid the groundwork for his love of learning.

Wolf graduated from high school in 1929 and studied music for one year at a conservatory in Berlin until July, 1930.In the summers between 1930 and 1933, he went to Berlin to study violin. After attending law school in Jena, he graduated as "konfidante" in 1933, but he was unable to practice law until such time as he completed an apprenticeship under the supervision of a licensed attorney. Due to the anti-semitic laws which were in place by that time, this was not possible. These laws prohibited Jews from practicing law, or being involved in medicine, teaching or banking. In 1933, Wolfgang left Germany and went to Paris but could not find work there, so the following year, he left Paris and went to Holland where his sister Elsi, a math teacher, was by this time married with two small children. She and her husband, a British citizen named Hans Danziger, planned to open a school in Holland. From July of 1934 until December of 1940, Wolf lived in den Haag and worked part-time in a book store in the Hauge Nieuwendijk (which no longer exists). It was there that he met Afra Geiger, a Jewish woman some twenty years his senior. One can only speculate about the true nature of their relationship, whether she was his Muse or his mentor, friend or lover. His attraction to Afra was due in part to her self-assurance and intelligence. Prior to moving to The Hague, she had been part of the inner circle of the eminent German philosopher Karl Jaspers. Coming from such a rarefied environment, she was an accomplished older woman with a confidence that was, no doubt, intriguing and reassuring to young Wolf.

In May of 1940, when the Germans invaded Holland, killing 20,000 people and ordering all Jews to leave coastal areas, Wolfgang and Afra moved to the small town of Driebergen. Because there was a town ordinance that required new residents to register, the

local news had an "Incoming" section that listed
"Wolfgang Herschkowitsch—violinist." Two local
musicians—Anton ("Ton") Akkerman, violinist, and Dr.
van Dongen, dentist and pianist, contacted Wolf, and
they began playing together. In turn, Ton contacted his
friend Johanna, telling her that "a new guy with a
funny name was in town and wanted to play quartets,"
so she often joined them. Their friendship flourished
but, by 1941, the situation had deteriorated; refugees
who could leave, did. Their violist, Lou Tas, left in the
fall of 1941 via Portugal en route to England where he
joined the allied military. In January of 1942, Wolfgang
decided to attempt the same daring escape. He made
contact with the same guide who accompanied the
violist and left with two other Jewish men, but they
were all caught. Wolf stayed in jail in Antwerp for
several weeks, then was transferred to Scheveningen—
the "Orange Hotel"—where he was given a sentence of
three months for border crossing. There was no
mention made of his being Jewish. After he was
released in April of 1942, he received a notice to report
to the detention camp in Westerbork to be put on a
transport to a concentration camp. The Akkerman
family suggested that he hide at their house. Ton, Otto,
and their mother lived at Burgermeesterlaan 10 in
Driebergen, where he stayed until May of 1945, more
than three years. Only once did he go outside, and that
was to a dentist who was a member of the Dutch
Underground, dedicated to helping the Jews. There
were two other men in hiding there in the attic which
was partitioned off so they could have some semblance
of privacy. There was only one pot-bellied stove in the
whole house, and the roof was thatched, so they
suffered terribly during those three years, especially in
the winter when it is bitterly cold in Holland. Because
he had to stay upstairs during the daytime, Wolf

studied Russian and played a muted fiddle to pass the time. Johanna would later remark to me that it was "because of his temperament that he was able to endure the isolation of those terrible years." She knew others who did not have the self-discipline to get through the ordeal, went outside and were caught.

Wolfgang, in an undated photo, practicing violin.

As for Afra, her mother was Jewish; her father was Catholic, and they were German. She was highly educated and apparently had come from a privileged upbringing. Afra had been a philosophy student of great promise. She was a close associate of Karl Jaspers, the acclaimed German psychologist/ philosopher, and his inner circle of academicians. In 1920, she applied to study under Edmund Husserl, the renowned phenomenologist, but when he found out, he supposedly blocked her from being accepted. It had nothing to do with her being Jewish, because he was raised in a Jewish household himself. Instead, it was his opposition to her gender. He was, allegedly, adamantly opposed to women becoming philosophy professors. Husserl's rejection of Afra sparked a confrontation between him and Jaspers in Freiburg and affected their long-term friendship.

At the time that Wolf met her, she was working in den Haag for a man who sold antique books, a member of the Gottschalk family. Once they were ordered to leave the coast, she went with Wolf to Driebergen where they became active in helping to find hiding places for other Jews. She was assisting an elderly, blind Jewish woman when she was apparently betrayed by someone and was caught. In 1944, she was picked up; from the train enroute to Westerbork, she threw a postcard addressed to Wolf at Johanna's address: Oosthuiselaan 4 in Driebergen. It was written in veiled language to protect herself and Wolf, and at Westerbork, she was allowed to write a few times. Unfortunately, none of the letters seem to have survived the war; it would be interesting to know her thoughts at the time. No one knew which camp she was transferred to since Westerbork was only a distribution point, but Wolf later learned she got typhoid fever at Ravensbruck in Germany—a notorious camp for women and children. This letter was written by Wolfgang to a mutual friend after the war:

> "Dear Mrs. Herzfeld,
>
> Perhaps you may remember me. I was a good friend of Erick (Kohnke); we played music together often in Scheveningen, and once I actually sat in your little car when you took me home one evening. I lived at that time with my sister Elsi Danziger in Havenkade. Do you recall? This letter is an answer to your letter of May 25 about Afra Geiger. It came into my hands in the following way. I met Afra in April 1938 through Erick. We quickly became good friends and lived together first in den Haag (the Hague) and later here until I had to go 'underground' because of the Jewish 'razzias' (round-ups). In the meantime, Afra moved to the

above address (on the Kraaijbeeklaan) and I moved again into her room. Afra herself was arrested in July because she had taken in an elderly, blind Jewish woman. Since she is 'half Jewish,' she was taken to Westerbork, and from there, transported to Germany. I have not yet heard from her. You are sure to understand how horrible that is for me.

Unfortunately, I can give you no good news. From Leni and Erick I have heard nothing. Also, her mother became a victim. Afra placed her with a lady here and everything was going well until suddenly, the lady needed an operation and so she had to close her house because it was impossible to leave her mother there alone or all the neighbors and suppliers would become accessories. Her mother went to Zeist (5k from here) and there she was apparently betrayed by someone. That was in December of '43 or January of '44. I remember exactly that Afra at that time already sat in prison but was allowed to go free, since there was no evidence that she had knowingly taken in a Jewess. The address in Zeist, I believe, belonged to a lady here. The (Dutch) Jewish information bureau— Weteringschans 104, Amsterdam, has now begun to publish lists of the names of those who were saved. These lists refer to all Jews, regardless of nationality. Except for the most recent, I have examined all of the lists but have discovered no acquaintances on them. Rest assured that I will write to you as soon as I see or hear something.

Anneke (the daughter of the Kohnkes) has gotten through this terrible time in good health. She was and is living at the home of Mr. Ing. J. Blacquiere, Hofwijckstraat 46, Voorburg (Z.H.). Afra often visited the people to reassure herself of the welfare of the child. I would also like to see the child, but at the moment, it is impossible because the trains are not yet running. I can't use my bicycle either because the tires are completely flat.

Since this is a common complaint, I also can't
borrow a bike. When at some point an opportunity
presents itself, I will do it and write to you then. It
causes me eternal sorrow that I must give you such
sad news and you may be certain of my feelings
even if I can't express it. How could one find such
words   for   it?   Unfortunately,   I   need   little
imagination in order to know how you feel since I
lost not only Afra but also my sister Elsi and her
children were taken. Nevertheless, we dare not lose
hope.   The   lists   appear   slowly   and   are
understandably not complete since they are based
in large part on private communication. So it is that
I, who am safe, appear on no list. Live well.
Heartfelt greetings from yours,

W.H."

Kraaljbeeklaan 4

Sehr verehrte Frau Herzfeld:

Vielleicht erinnern Sie sich meiner noch. Ich war ein guterFreund von rich(Kohnke), wir haben in Scheveningen viel zusammen musiziert, und einmal habe ich auch in Ihrem kleinen Auto gesessen, als Sie mich eines Abends nach Hause brachten. Ich wohnte damals bei meiner Schwest ter Ilsi Danziger in der Havenkade. Sagt Ihnen das etwas? Dieser Brief ist eine Antwort Ihres Briefes vom 25. Mai an Afra Geiger geschrieben. Er kam auf folge de Weise in meine Hände. Ich lernte Afr x April 1938 bei Erich kennen, wir wurden schnell sehr gut befreun et und haben dann im Haag, später hier immer zusammen gewohnt, bis ch wegen der Judenrazzias anderswo "untertauchen" musste. In der Tischenzeit ist Afra nach der obenstehenden Adresse umgezogen, und n wohne ich wieder in einem ihrer Zimmer. Afra selbst ist im Juli v rigen Jahres verhaftet worden, weil sie eine alte blinde jüdische ie zu sich genommen hatte. Da sie selbst "Halbjüdin" ist, wurde sie h esterbork gebracht und von dort nach Deutschland verschleppt; habe noch nichts von ihr gehört. Sie werden am besten begreifen, schrecklich das für mich ist............. Leider kann ich Ihnen keine guten Nachrichten geben. Von Leni und h habe ich noch nichts gehört. Und auch Ihre mutter hat de... .... Afra hatte sie hier bei einer allein-

An excerpt from Wolf's post-war letter to Frau Herzfeld about Afra Geiger.

As I read this letter and learned of his obvious affection for the child that he and Afra were so concerned about, it made me wonder if Delia somehow reminded him of the little girl that he was so anxious to see. That he was able to reconnect with her—even if in a vicarious way—perhaps brought some solace to his tormented last years. I recall being so amazed that, on the occasion of Delia's first birthday, Wolfgang, who still rather resented me, actually drove to our little apartment off of Forest Lane in north Dallas to spend the afternoon with her, bringing her several gifts and laughing at her childish antics. When she was born, I was somewhat surprised that she looked so much like Wolf, and she blossomed into a real beauty with thick, curly, red hair and a delightful disposition. As cancer progressively robbed him of his strength, Delia would accompany me to visit him and never failed to bring a smile to his face. For those brief times, it seemed that he was able to transcend the pain to enjoy the little granddaughter that he loved so much.

According to Johanna, Afra's father had been well-known, perhaps as an artist, and she had some valuable possessions which she distributed before the situation deteriorated completely and they were forced to leave the coastal region. One massive armoire is reportedly in a museum in den Haag, and a sculpture was given to a man in New York for safekeeping, but I have been unable to confirm this. She also owned property in Bildhoven, but since Afra left no will and Wolf wasn't a relative, the property was apparently claimed by the state. Wolf kept a picture of Afra and her older sister, painted by their father, and Johanna sold other paintings after his death at an auction and gave the money to the Akkerman family in gratitude for saving Wolf's life. What a lot of people don't understand is that many Jewish people were forced to leave behind everything that was dear to them—not just homes, furniture, and jewelry, but mementoes—family photos, marriage certificates, graduation plaques. Trying to reconstruct history with no documents is difficult. The fact that Wolf was able to keep the painting of Afra and her sister all those years demonstrates its—and her—importance to him. It is mind-boggling and heart-wrenching to realize that people were treated in such an inhumane way and that they literally had nothing at the end of the war to prove their family history—if they survived at all.

The painting of Afra Geiger and her sister,
painted by their father.

CHAPTER FOUR
THE WAR YEARS

When ninety-eight percent of Dutch university students refused to sign an oath of allegiance to the German government at the end of 1943, the Germans weren't happy and closed the universities in retaliation. Many of the students, including Johanna, had to go into hiding themselves when the government issued a general summons for them to report to work camps. Johanna went into hiding at her friend Nell Blinck's home in the center of Holland, out in the country. She, of course, traveled by bike. The good news was, that she knew by that time that Wolf was safe. Since mid-1942, she had heard nothing from him and knew better than to ask. The fewer people who knew, the less risk there was of getting caught. So the night before she left for Nell's, she was invited to the Akkerman's home to spend the night—for safety reasons, she thought. Once she got there, they had dinner, and about eight o'clock, they said, "We have a surprise for you!" Ton Akkerman then went to the foot of the stairs leading to the attic, whistled a few bars from Mozart's "Hunt Quartet," and Wolfgang came down for a joyous reunion! Until then, she only knew from their dentist, Dr. van Dongen, that Wolf was "safe."

Interestingly, I recently recalled that Johanna had given me a book years ago entitled *Geboren am Blauen Montag* by Karl Grebe. I vaguely remembered her mentioning that there was something about Wolf in it. Upon investigation, I found that his book also tells the story about this reunion. Like Wolf, he had been born in Jena, Germany; they had a long-term friendship and had kept in touch over the years. In his book, Karl

Grebe lamented the early death of his friend, Wolf.

In the meantime, Johanna had been busy, along with her parents, sister and cousin Jan, doing whatever she could to assist with the "Dutch Underground," which was very active because of the vast numbers of people in hiding. It was made more difficult because the German military had confiscated their blankets, radiators, food, bikes, batteries, radios, anything that would make life a little easier for the Dutch people. Of course, war is hell, but Johanna often said that funny things happened, too. She once remarked to me, "Jan and I were young, and so we still saw humor in a lot of things." I think it would be hard not to laugh and have a good time when Jan—Johanna's favorite cousin—was around. I once used him as the subject of an assignment for a creative writing class that I was taking at the University of North Texas. The instructor, a local columnist and author named A.C. Greene who wrote about Texas history, had told us to write about a "memorable character." I wrote, "Hardly a day goes by that I don't think of Jan van Dam, who was, undoubtedly, the most colorful gentleman whom I have ever been blessed to know. In 1970, during my first visit to my now ex-husband's Dutch relatives, I met Jan, who at that time was sixty-eight years old, although he was completely unaware of that fact. He was the youngest senior citizen I have ever met, because he had the pure heart and the receptive mind of an eighteen-year-old. Perhaps this was due to his lifelong bachelor status and his constant association with young people in his role as an instructor of mathematics at a Montessori school in Driebergen, Holland. Young people sought him out as a mentor, even after his retirement. They frequently had parties at his large, old home, which they conspired to maintain with annual repairs and paint jobs as well as monthly cleanings.

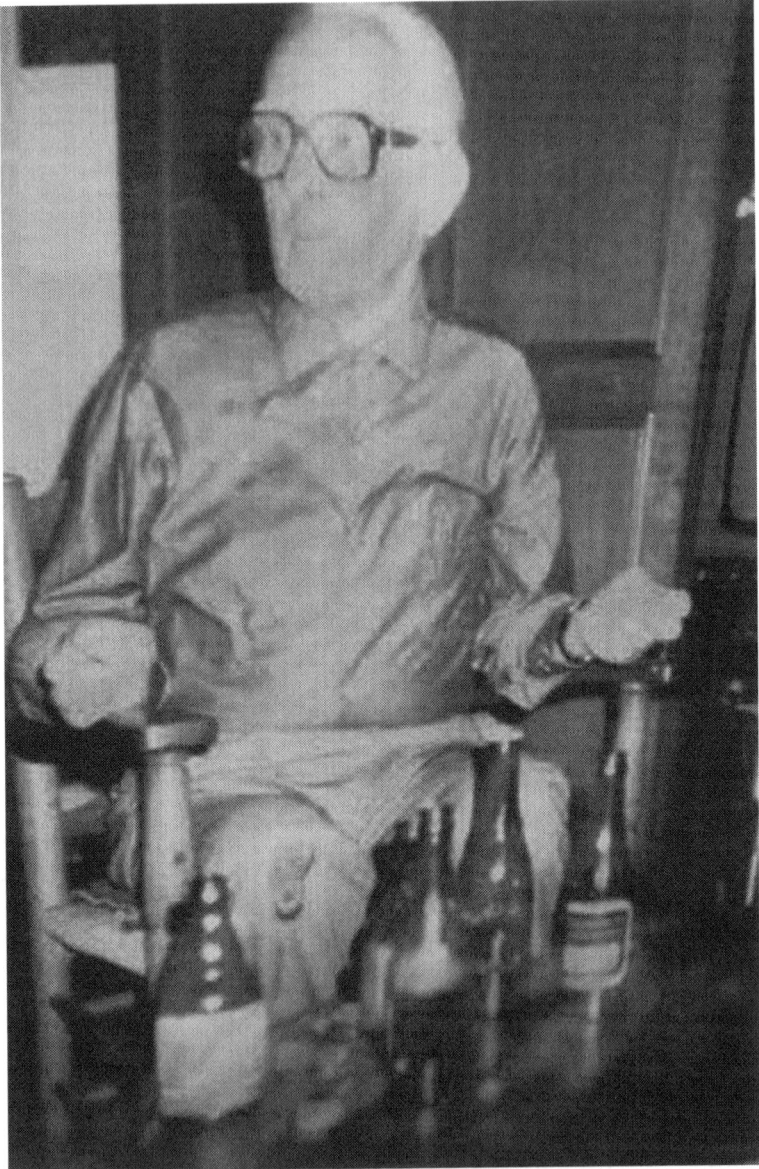

"Om" Jan van Dam
with an assortment of his favorite beverages.

During World War II, Jan had been a member of
the Dutch resistance, which he served with enthusiasm

and courage, if not always promptness. It was reported, as a tribute to his absent-minded reputation, that he had once missed a critical 8:00 PM meeting, only to appear at 11:00 PM to announce that he could not make it at 8:00 PM. I attribute one of my most harrowing experiences to his penchant for driving his cigar-smoke-blackened VW at high speeds along treacherous, lonely canal roads in the wee hours of the morning. During these trips, he was the consummate conversational gentleman, rarely turning his attention away from me, his anxiety-ridden companion, to look at the narrow road, which sloped down to water on both sides.

Jan was the little boy who never grew up. This earned him much criticism from some of his peers, who were infuriated by his carefree, happy-go-lucky, irresponsible approach to life. This same carefree nature happened to earn him the love, respect and warmest regard of a series of younger generations, who pledged to care for him and prayed that he would live forever.

He didn't, of course, but before he died in 1986, he made his only visit to the United States. My last memory of him is captured in a photograph, enshrined on my wall, in which he is smiling broadly, as usual, surrounded by a field of Texas bluebonnets. It hangs above an empty tin cigar box from his extensive collection. In accordance with his request—a characteristic of his desire to be of service to people, even in death—his body was donated to the medical branch of Amsterdam's Frei Universitat."

Jan was the son of Piet van Dam, who was also a math teacher. When his close friend, Caroline ten Brueckenkarte passed away, he inherited her house on Oosthuiselaan, just a few doors away from Johanna's sister and mother. This was where we stayed on our

first visit to Holland in 1970. I soon learned that, while
he was Johanna's favorite cousin, he was far from the
favorite of her sister Lida. She disliked Jan for his free-
wheeling, non-conventional lifestyle and had furious
confrontations with him on several occasions. I
gathered that the animosity had gone on for years, as
far back as their childhood, but, during the war,
everyone worked together to accomplish a common
goal.

Om Jan's specialty was growing tobacco. Both
Johanna and Jan were smokers at the time. She gave
up the habit sometime in the 60's, but Jan was a
lifelong smoker. She said that once, he had a
particularly nice crop of tobacco growing and was
eagerly awaiting his harvest, but she couldn't wait. She
went out and picked some leaves and put them in the
oven (right before the Germans shut off the gas) and
had a very enjoyable, if surreptitious, time smoking.
Later, Om Jan said, "Something funny is going on. My
plants were beautiful, but now they are so sparse, I
think someone's been in them." He never suspected
her, his favorite cousin and confidante. She laughed
and confessed. He, of course, forgave her, but he kept
close surveillance on subsequent crops. They could
sometimes buy tobacco for five hundred gulden (the
price of a small cookie tin) from the black market. It
was decent tobacco, and you could bribe people for it
and with it. Once, during an "eten halen" (a trek to the
country to load up on vegetables and provisions), in the
northeast part of Holland, she returned with things
from her father's dairy friends. She had milk powder
and butter, among other things, but to get back home,
she had to cross the Esel River near Zwollen and was
confronted by Germans who accused her of
transporting food. This was forbidden under German
law, and she was terrified. She escaped being arrested

because she happened to have some tobacco with her and used it to bribe them. Although she hated giving up the tobacco, she knew that her freedom was worth it.

Johanna's specialty seemed to be smuggling things to people in hiding. To that end, she had a big winter coat with secret pockets to hide ration cards, letters and, sometimes, cigarettes. In the winter of 1944, she was smuggling a letter that was for a friend in hiding when she was stopped by a German for wearing a yellow daisy pin on her coat; the daisy was a symbol of their Princess Margarethe of the House of Orange. The German began yelling at her and cursing her and was about to grab the pin from her lapel when she abruptly took it off and handed it to him. "Here, take it," she said fiercely. The idea of his touching her was so repulsive, she absolutely recoiled from the thought. And once again, she felt lucky to have gotten away. Had they discovered the contraband hidden in her coat, she would have gone straight to jail. During that winter, she traveled repeatedly between Driebergen and den Haag in snow and ice, frequently carrying letters. The Dutch Underground had developed a system of code words on the letters to avoid the Germans identifying names and addresses in the event that they were intercepted.

Of course, the war was brutal and affected everybody, but the winter of 1944-45 was so harsh, the Dutch dubbed it "the Hunger Winter." In September—October of 1944, the Dutch railroads went on strike because they were being used to take food to Germany and refused to continue to participate in the starvation of their own people. The Germans were using thrashing machines to reap barley, but ninety percent went to Germany, while only ten percent was allotted to the farmers. If they had half a loaf of bread a week, they felt fortunate. After a while, the farmers began to keep up with where the thrashing machines were located, and they would get up at 3:00 AM in order to beat the Germans to the day's haul. And, even then, the barley was horrible. It was, literally, the dregs of the crop, withered and full of sticks. Her Uncle Nic had died when she was only fourteen, and Johanna still had his motorcycle coat. She traded it for five hundred pounds of oats, part of which she gave away to elderly people in Driebergen. The oats weren't refined and stuck in her throat. They were also loaded with mice droppings; Johanna and Lida would pick out the mice pellets, then grind the oats in a meat grinder. As bad as the oats were, it kept them alive for quite a long time. Once, she traded six dish towels for ten pounds of dried green peas. Other people were trading linens, jewelry and silver from dowries for food. Delia recalls, however, that her Oma once told her that many people buried their good silver and other valuables in their backyards to hide them from the Germans who were notorious for confiscating anything that they could send back to Germany or sell on the Black Market. Because their stash of buried family treasure was never discovered, several pieces still remain in the van Dam family. Others weren't so lucky and lost everything, including beautiful, valuable family heirlooms.

People in the country fared better than their counterparts in the city who literally starved to death because they had no access to even the meager vegetables that were left behind in the fields by the Germans. Johanna often alluded to the many times that she and Jan would go out in the freezing cold in the middle of the night to root around in the dirt for rotten potatoes. Even rotten food was better than no food.

At one point, a troop of Germans was sequestered in the forest right across from Johanna's house in Driebergen. The Kraybeeklaan around the corner was full of Germans, who Johanna described as "dilapidated," because at this point, toward the end of the war, supplies and fresh uniforms were scarce, and the Germans began to look the worse for wear. Some of them proved to be at least somewhat accommodating on occasion. Because of the blackout , the Dutch citizens had to charge batteries by getting on stationary bikes or, if they were in the country, they would use windmills. But Johanna asked the Germans in the nearby forest if they would charge her battery, and she was flabbergasted when they actually did it! By this time, the Germans were tired and just wanted to go home. It was only two months before Holland's liberation, and everyone knew the end was near, including the Germans. One morning, Johanna's mother Nellie set out on her bicycle to run some errands. She hadn't gotten very far when she was hijacked by a young German soldier who very apologetically stole her bike. When she got home, she was so chagrined by the experience that the rest of the family had to laugh. "Imagine," she said, "he took my bike away." But she also told them that the young guy had said, "I just need a way home."

Together, Jan and Johanna's specialty was cutting down pine trees for fuel. Naturally, it was difficult, because, when the trees fell, they made an unmistakable sound. In the dead of winter, between 5:00 and 8:00 PM, when it was pitch black, they would go into the forest and work as quietly as possible until the tree fell. The work was slow and tedious under horrible conditions. Their equipment left much to be desired since the Germans had taken most of their good tools. As soon as the tree had fallen, they ran back home and waited breathlessly in case someone had heard the noise and gone to investigate. Once they were confident that the coast was clear, they slipped back to the site, chopped up the tree into manageable chunks and carried it away, piece by piece, which took most of the night. In winter, at night especially, Holland is bitterly cold. I can't even imagine the courage and fortitude it took for them to perform this ritual, knowing that Germans might appear at any moment. While they kept much of the wood for their own use, a lot of it was distributed to the elderly people in their little corner of Driebergen. The degree of this quiet heroism is amazing to me. Johanna's practical and resolute approach in defying danger so that she could help others makes me wonder if I would have the courage to confront evil in such a direct way. She is, quite simply, an inspiration to me and an angel to everyone who benefited from her strength.

May 7, 1945: Liberation Day in Holland. It was also Johanna's twenty-sixth birthday. For two days after the Liberation, there was an "eerie silence," Johanna recalls. It was the calm after the storm. After Prince Bernhard of the Netherlands signed the Armistice in Edam, the Germans "just disappeared like snow." She saw Wolf immediately during the two "quiet" days. They visited, reminisced, played music, and then she got seriously ill. Because her resistance was low, she had developed what the Dutch termed "angina," but which in English is strep throat. For four weeks, she was sick and isolated; her doctor had told her to avoid crowds or she would likely develop tuberculosis.

A Canadian postcard widely distributed after the war.

After things settled down, Johanna and Wolf had decisions to make, and, of course, they relished their new freedom after years of a miserable existence—especially Wolf. Being confined for so long had been a hardship for him, as it was for everyone in his position. But now, he was completely and unequivocally free!

After she recuperated from the angina, Johanna went back to school to study chemistry. She noted that many people of her generation ended up doing something other than what they had set out to do. She, for example, had studied chemistry but ended up playing cello professionally. The law career that Wolf had envisioned was also derailed, and he, too, became a professional musician. The most important thing was that they were alive. By the fall of 1945, Wolf's family was working to get him to the United States. Sponsorship was mandatory, and the volumes of paperwork were time-consuming, but they were determined. At that time, the quota for Germans emigrating to the U.S. was overfilled; the quota was large, and it was still early after the war. Wolf's mother

knew the right people in New York to get sponsorship
for him; her cousin, Betty Colquin, had sponsored her
with the help of New York Senator Jacob Javitts. In the
meantime, Johanna continued with her studies, and
Wolf was translating for the Canadians in the
aftermath of the war. He also got a job with the Utrecht
Symphony. In June of 1946, Johanna went to
Switzerland for a couple of months for her health, but
by that time, she and Wolf had begun to talk about
marriage...eventually. She said that there was "no
formal proposal; it was just a gradual thing." They
married in February of 1947. At the time, she was living
in the same house with Wolf—two houses away from
Oosthuiselaan on the Kraybeeklaan. The emigration
papers for Wolf had already been filed, so the process
for Johanna had to be started. After months of waiting,
their visas were finally approved in May of 1947. In
August, they boarded a freighter – either the "Edam" or
the "Leerdam," a two hundred passenger ship with the
Holland-America Line. The trip cost one hundred-
eighty Dutch Gulden per person, which was paid by the
Hebrew Immigration Assistance Service. The ship was
segregated by males and females—dormitory-style.
They arrived in Philadelphia on the fourteenth of
August, 1947. It was 104 degrees. The line at the
immigration center was long, and Johanna began to
feel faint. She had that Dutch way of becoming very
flushed in the heat. For her, this hot weather was
unprecedented, and the long trip had exhausted her.
She recalled that a kind, Black man noticed her
distress and, fearing that she was about to be
overcome with heat exhaustion, came over to her and
showed her where she could get a drink of water. That
simple act of kindness was something that touched her
deeply; she never forgot her good Samaritan on that
first day in a new country.

As for Wolfgang's sisters, Elsi, the math teacher, had married a British citizen who was also Jewish, but because their children had been born in London, they thought they were safe. Sadly, they were mistaken. Because they had once been picked up in Holland and detained, but later released, they had a false sense of security. Johanna and others had advised them to go into hiding, but they did not and were eventually picked up. None of them survived the war. Another sister, Rosa, stayed in Germany because she was in a "mixed marriage." Her husband, Fritz Oberdoerffer, had studied music at the University of Jena in 1919, which is most likely where he met Rosa. He was not Jewish. In fact, Johanna recalled that he was, prior to the war, in German military service. They had one daughter, Marianne (Nonni). During World War II, all three were forced to work in a labor camp. They stayed in Berlin until the end of the war and eventually emigrated to the United States, where Fritz became an acclaimed professor of musicology at the University of Texas in Austin. The third sister, Yela, had left Germany with her husband and young son in 1934 or '35 to go to Czechoslovakia. From there, they went to the United States in 1937 or '38, under the same sponsorship as Wolf's mother. They settled in New York where they established a successful psychiatric practice.

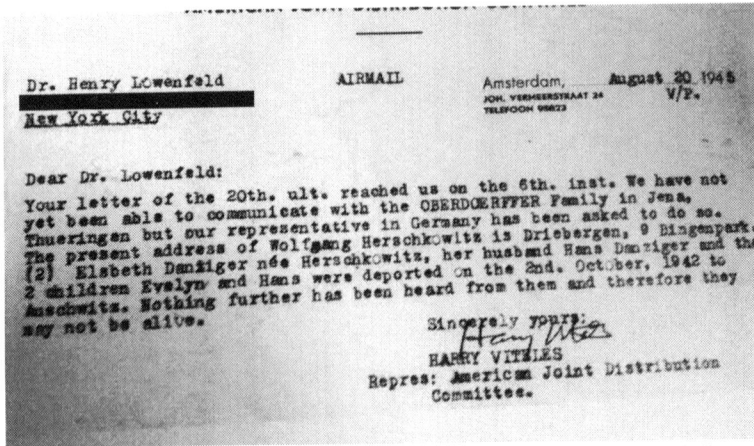

Dr. Henry Lowenfeld   AIRMAIL   Amsterdam,   August 20, 1945
                                                JOH. VERMEERSTRAAT 24   V/P.
New York City   TELEFOON 98873

Dear Dr. Lowenfeld:
Your letter of the 20th. ult. reached us on the 6th. inst. We have not
yet been able to communicate with the OBERDOERFFER Family in Jena,
Thueringen but our representative in Germany has been asked to do so.
The present address of Wolfgang Herschkowitz is Driebergen, 9 Bingenpark.
[2] Elsbeth Danziger née Herschkowitz, her husband Hans Danziger and the
2 children Evelyn and Hans were deported on the 2nd. October, 1942 to
Auschwitz. Nothing further has been heard from them and therefore they
may not be alive.

                                   Sincerely yours:

                                   HARRY VITELES
                         Repres: American Joint Distribution
                                   Committee.

The telegram announcing the presumed deaths of the
Danziger Family

Anaeta's story was, perhaps, the most dramatic. Wolf's mother had stayed in Germany until the fall of 1940. Because she was born in Russia, she was able to return there and traveled with a group, assisted by the Hebrew Immigration Assistance Service (HIAS). This tiny woman, not even five feet tall, a widow aged sixty-two, traveled alone to Siberia via the Trans-Siberian Railway, then to Kobe, Japan, where she boarded the *Hie Maru* to Seattle, Washington, then went to New York via train, arriving in 1941. The trip took three weeks. That this little lady was able to set out on this epic journey all alone to start a new life in a new country is nothing short of amazing. But having lost her husband eight years earlier and with the advent of war looming, she had little choice but to go. On arriving in Seattle, she indicated that she would be staying with her daughter Helene (Yela) Lowenfeld in New York. On April 1, 1946, she petitioned for naturalization as a U.S. citizen, concluding an amazing journey for this courageous woman.

An excerpt from Anaeta's letter at the beginning of her journey to the United States

Still another example of Anaeta's courage occurred in 1935. The incident involved her son-in-law, Heinrich Lowenfeld, who was married to her daughter Yela. Heinrich's father, Raphael Lowenfeld, had been chosen by Leo Tolstoy's editor, Eugen Diederichs, to translate Tolstoy's literary works into German. Diederichs' two sons took over the publishing company, and, in 1935, they stopped paying royalties on Lowenfeld's Tolstoy translations to his three children, including Heinrich. They were confident that no one would challenge the right of an Aryan company to deny payment to Jewish people. By that time, Hitler's laws barring Jews from participating in professional careers were firmly in place. But that did not stop Anaeta from attempting to challenge what she considered to be shameless discrimination. So the little widow paid a call on Peter Diederichs, not to ask him to do anything, but to shame him, because he would recall a time when her late husband and his father Eugen Diederichs were both highly respected citizens of Jena. The point was to let him know that he was "an impudent opportunist, to take advantage of the present situation to cheat people who are already in financial distress."

When I met Anaeta in the late '60's, she was living with Wolf and Johanna and was our frequent dinner companion. It was so funny to see this elderly lady, who spoke no English, admonish her child Wolfgang to eat his veggies and offer him tissues as if he were four years old. He chafed under her direction as if he WERE four years old, but he was always respectful. To me, she kindly offered her assistance at my attempts to learn German. She sat with me for long periods, pronouncing words of objects in a German picture book. I will never forget her kindness. Because Anaeta had snow white hair, Delia called her "Oma with the Old Hair," to distinguish her from her other Oma-Johanna- and the Dutch grandmother "Omama."

Initially, Wolf and Johanna stayed in New York with Anaeta until they could find an apartment. Johanna got a job teaching weaving to blind people at the Lighthouse of the Blind. While she taught them, they were, in turn, teaching her; she said that her English improved greatly during her time there. She had developed a passion for weaving during her youth in Norway and continued weaving well into her eighties. (Her loom filled the large bedroom at the back of the house in Dallas for many years.) Wolf was translating and wanted to audition for a symphony orchestra, but because of the union rules, he had to be a resident for six months before he could join the union and audition. In the fall of 1948, Wolf went to Indianapolis; she followed in December. But Wolf was not happy there; he called Indianapolis "a hole in the wall." By April of 1949, they had returned to New York. Wolf had gotten discouraged and wanted to return to Holland. In July of 1949, they returned to Holland, but they had had the foresight to secure "re-entry permits," enabling them to return within six months. Going through emigration at that point would have taken years. In Utrecht, Wolf got his old job back with the Utrecht Orchestra. As Johanna put it, "He got a job, and I got a baby." Their only son, Alex, was born on December 30, 1949. Ironically, by March of 1950, Wolf admitted that he had misgivings about leaving the U.S. He missed the "space and the vastness," which only makes sense, considering his years of confinement in the attic.

UTRECHTSCH STEDELIJK ORCHEST

Vrij van zegel ingevolge
art. 1637 ij B.W.

OVEREENKOMST

Tussen „HET UTRECHTSCH STEDELIJK ORCHEST" (afd. A van de Stichting Collegium Musicum Ultrajectinum, verder aangeduid als: „het orkest") gevestigd te Utrecht, ondergetekende ter ene zijde, en

HERSCHKOWITSCH, Wolfgang

ondergetekende ter andere zijde, wonende te   Driebergen , is aangegaan een arbeidsovereenkomst onder de volgende voorwaarden:

a. De ondergetekende ter andere zijde verbindt zich in het orkest mede te werken als

1e violist   (hoofdinstrument),   (bij-instrument)

en/of in dat orkest een zodanig ander instrument te bespelen of zodanige andere partij(en) te vervullen als de dirigent hem zal aanwijzen.

b. Het orkest verbindt zich voor de medewerking bedoeld onder a. aan de ondergetekende ter andere zijde te voldoen een honorarium ten bedrage van ƒ 2475.— per jaar, te betalen in bedragen van ƒ 206,25 per kalendermaand, na aftrek van de door hem/haar verschuldigde bijdragen, op de laatste van elke maand waarin het honorarium verdiend is. Valt deze datum op een Zon- of feestdag, dan geschiedt de betaling op de daaraanvoorafgaande werkdag. De wijze van betaling wordt door het Bestuur bepaald.

c. Beide ondergetekenden verbinden zich de verplichtingen na te komen, vermeld in onderstaande algemene voorwaarden.

d. Deze overeenkomst is aangegaan voor de tijd van 1 November 49 tot en met 31 Augustus 1950.

Indien zij niet door een der partijen en vóór de 1e Juni 1950 of van een der volgende jaren schriftelijk is opgezegd, is zij telkens onder dezelfde voorwaarden weer voor het volgende jaar verlengd.

Aldus gedaan en in duplo getekend, te Utrecht.

         1 November 1949.

Ondergetekende ter andere zijde: Ondergetekende ter ene zijde,
                                   Namens het Bestuur:

                                            Voorzitt

                                            Secreta

ALGEMENE VOORWAARDEN

bedoeld in de Overeenkomst tussen het U.S.O. (afd. A van het Collegium Musicum Ultrajecti en de leden van het orkest.

Art. 1. De orkestleden zijn verplicht hun diensten met ijver en nauwgezetheid te verv door hun gedragingen de naam der instelling, waaraan zij verbonden zijn, hoog te houden e overigens de belangen daarvan te bevorderen

De orkestleden zijn verplicht elkaar op aanwijzing van de dirigent of zijn plaatsvervang ziekte met hoofd- en bij-instrument te vervangen.

In bijzondere gevallen, ter beoordeling van het Bestuur, op voorstel van de Directe het vervangend lid deswege een bijzondere vergoeding kunnen worden toegekend.

Art. 2. Elk orkestlid is verplicht zijn diensten te verlenen op al zodanige tijden en pl eveneens op Zon- en feestdagen, en voor al zodanige uitvoeringen en repetities, alsmede z schikbaar te stellen voor de daartoe nodige reizen met de door het Bestuur aan te wijzen v middelen, en voor de verblijven elders, als het Bestuur nodig zal achten te bepalen.

In bijzondere gevallen, ter beoordeling van het Bestuur, zullen de orkestleden met le particulieren genoegen moeten nemen.

Bij het reizen moeten desgewenst alle kleinere instrumenten door de bespelers in het worden medegenomen. De grotere instrumenten worden vervoerd

Wolfgang's contract with the Utrecht Orchestra

Johanna and the baby stayed in Holland until December of 1950, but Wolf had returned in October to be available for auditions. He got two job offers: Minneapolis and Dallas. He chose Dallas because, as he once remarked, "I never want to be cold again," a reference to the extreme cold that he had endured during his years in the attic. The only heat in the house on Burgermeisterlaan had been the pot-bellied stove in the kitchen. My daughter and I have ridden bikes several times to see the house, and we noticed that it had a thatched roof on a visit in 1977, but we didn't realize that the roof was not for decoration only. We thought it was a nod to earlier times when, in fact, it was the only roof; the cold surely permeated it and chilled the inhabitants in the attic to the bone. So Wolf's lament was understandable, and his choice of Dallas, which heats up very nicely in the summer months, also obvious. For a while, they lived in a garage apartment on Swiss Avenue. Later, they moved to a house on Lindale which was near Sears where Wolf had taken a job on the loading docks to supplement his income with the Dallas Symphony Orchestra. This was necessary because the symphony only played twenty-three weeks out of a year. Of course, Wolf's law degree from Germany was no help to him in the U.S. Shortly after moving to New York in 1949, he had attended Brooklyn School of Law briefly, but didn't complete the studies there. The German government compensated him for the loss of his profession with a lump sum payment of five thousand Deutsch Marks. Only German citizens were compensated; Hungarian Jews, for example, could not claim the restitution. This "Wiedergutmachung" had been established at Nuremburg immediately after the war. Wolfgang's mother, Anaeta, also qualified to receive the compensation.

In 1951 or '52, during an "orchestra crisis" in Dallas, Johanna and Wolf took Alex and went by train to San Antonio for a music job. While there, she drafted maps for a company that did aerial surveys. She thought it was an interesting job, and it paralleled her interest in geography. They lived in an adobe house on Goliad St. within walking distance of the Alamo. She recalled that the termites were horrible, so after one season, they returned to Dallas. There, Wolf got a job as a bookkeeper for Liberty Steel. It was mindless, repetitive work, but it paid the bills. In the fall of 1957, she returned to the Dallas Symphony Orchestra; he followed suit in the fall of 1958. Because the pay in the DSO was so dismal, they both had jobs on the side. He continued working as a bookkeeper; she worked as a secretary for a doctor because of her medical vocabulary and knowledge of chemistry. From 1953-55, she also worked for Reserve Insurance Company doing claim work.

In 1955, she wanted to take Alex to visit her parents and asked for a leave of absence but was told that, upon her return, her benefits would have to start all over. She went anyway, returning in the spring of 1956 when they bought a house on a tree-lined street in Dallas where they lived for many years, often hosting casual gatherings of symphony members. It was a small "cottage-style" home, but they added a huge room on the back and converted the garage into a sitting room. It was very European in style and ambience. Wolf worked at Southern Methodist University during this time, occasionally translating, when he decided to get his master's degree in German with a minor in French, so he could teach. The topic of his thesis was Georg Buchner; unfortunately, it was then that he was first diagnosed with cancer, and his battle with the dreaded disease took precedence over his master's degree.

In early summer of 1968, when I was required to quit work six weeks before my baby was due, Wolf "hired" me to type his translations of applications that European chefs were sending to Dallas in anticipation of the opening of the new Fairmont Hotel. He paid me five dollars an hour, which was a good sum at the time, and I was glad to have a little extra income with a baby on the way. The applications for sous chef and master chef were interesting, with the aura of exoticism detailed in their resumes.

Johanna's sketch of Wolfgang was a matter of geometry,
she said.

CHAPTER FIVE
THE NEXT GENERATION

On my first trip to Europe in 1970, Delia was not quite two years old. Johanna was eager for her mother and sister to see Delia, and she underwrote the trip. I had never flown before; nor had I ever been out of the country. I didn't have a clue. My husband, on the other hand, had spent his summers in Holland visiting his relatives. Do you think he might have given me a "heads-up" about the weather or what to pack? There was no Google at the time, and I had no idea how to research the climate in Holland in the summer, so, in my naiveté, I packed everything! I had two big suitcases for a two week stay, plus Delia's suitcase. And everything in those suitcases was all wrong! Because Texas is so hot, I made the leap of faith that Holland would be, too. Was I ever wrong! This was way before global warming, and when we landed at Frankfurt's international airport, I felt like I had stepped back into winter! After Johanna met us at the airport, we spent a few hours on the road, driving in a rented red BMW en route to Holland. I was captivated by the beautiful scenery, the magnificent castles, the old-world architecture. One of the first things I saw was an honest-to-goodness, old-style chimney sweeper— straight out of Mary Poppins! It seemed so surreal; I was absolutely enchanted.

Because German laws prohibited children from riding in the front seat, Delia was not a happy camper. She wanted to be in the passenger seat next to her daddy, where she always traveled at home. Instead, she had to sit in the back with her Oma, and nothing could distract her from her absolute indignation at not getting to ride in the front! We spent the night in

Gondorf, a village on the Mosel River, and I remember sitting on the terrace of the restaurant and watching the fog roll in down the river. It literally looked like a cloud wall coming right at us. For dinner, we feasted on spargel (white asparagus – a German delicacy) and beef tenderloin, which was fabulous. We walked around the small town on the cobblestone streets and explored the chapel on the hotel's grounds. To me, it was like a dream. That night, when we went to bed, I encountered down comforters for the first time in my life. Like everything else I had experienced that day, it was amazing. I wasn't too thrilled about the bathrooms being down the hall, but at least I was prepared for that, unlike the clothing fiasco. Nothing could have dampened my enthusiasm.

The next morning, we departed for Driebergen and the family. En route, we stopped at a gas station in Holland, where we were met by adolescent boys who goose-stepped around the BMW, giving the stiff-armed Hitler salute. I was appalled and asked why they would do such a thing. The response was, "The car is registered in Germany, with the 'D' for Deutschland, and these boys are Dutch kids." Okay, but these kids weren't alive in the 1940's, so I wondered why they would do something so disrespectful. "Because," I was told, "old grudges die hard." So, twenty-five years after the war ended, the stories of the war kept alive by the parents were having a profound impact on these children. We exchanged the car for one with Holland's registration.

While some fine details have surely been lost in the mists of time, several things from that visit do stand out. In Driebergen, we were met warmly by Omama and Tante (aunt) Lida, who had gone overboard to insure that their dear Delia would be entertained. In their garden, they had created a sandbox with a pail and shovel and toys designed to keep her amused. Not that we would be spending that much time there. Our two weeks was packed with visits to friends and relatives and excursions.

Delia, aged two, playing in her Dutch sandbox.

Omama and Tante Lida lived on Oosthuiselaan, two doors away from Johanna's favorite cousin, Jan van Dam. That is where we stayed during our visit. He lived in a grand old house, and we were given the upstairs bedroom with a huge bathroom, and a wonderful old claw-footed bathtub. Om (uncle) Jan was such fun! He always had a cigar going; the ceiling of his old Volkswagen was black from cigar smoke. He was a wonderful host, anxious to please and very accommodating. His English was good, but he had no confidence in it, and so he came across as a slightly confused, absent-minded professor. But that demeanor was misleading. He was a brilliant math teacher, and many of his former students were frequent visitors to his home. He was a bit of a connoisseur when it came to beer. Each spring, he made the trek to Belgium for "Trappist" beer, made by the Trappist monks in their monastery. He always made sure that there was a variety of beer on hand, and he was eager to share his knowledge of beer with company. He also like aged Gouda cheese, so aged it felt like the cheese was biting you, instead of vice versa. Together, he said the beer and the cheese were perfectly complementary. Still, I preferred the "young" Gouda and still do to this day. Om Jan liked for things to be "natural," so he allowed his garden to grow as it wanted, which yielded pleasant surprises. He loved to show visitors the unusual flowers that were growing wild, including foxglove, which he proudly noted, is the source for digitalis. On one of our later visits to his home, when Delia was about eleven, he woke her up on the morning of her birthday—the fourth of July—with wild raspberries from his garden. She was very pleased and touched by his thoughtfulness. To this day, I honor that memory by giving her raspberries on her birthday.

Staying in Driebergen was like stepping back

into the past. It was delightful. The grandmother's house was filled with wonderful family heirlooms and antiques—magnificent armoires, roll-top desks, dining room furniture—all filled with old-world charm and the cachet of having been in the family , in some cases, for generations. After Omama passed away and Tante Lida sold the house, a few highly treasured pieces made their way to Dallas—at a hefty cost. Seeing them floods me with memories of the first visit. Coming from a country fixated on the newest and the shiniest and being transported to a place where the old and traditional are revered resonated with me. The history behind each piece—from the "sekretar" which had belonged to the brother who died young to the old eyeglasses and the pressed flowers on the hand-crocheted doilies—was so rich and striking, I couldn't help but fall in love with the place, and it reminds me now of what Bette Midler once said about London: "If it's 4:00 PM in New York, it's still 1939 in London." Holland had the same timeless ambience. When we woke up in the morning, we could smell the fresh bread from the bakery around the corner. Delia and I would walk to the bakery, buy a loaf of fresh farmer's bread, take it back to Jan's house and slather it with butter while it was still warm. "Lekker," as the Dutch say. Once, while driving down a rural road, we were stopped by shepherds guiding a herd of sheep across the road. Things like that just did not happen where I came from! And the rich aroma of fresh cow manure always elicited an excited squeal of appreciation from Johanna; she loved it because it reminded her of the time she spent with her father when he did his dairy research. She would always inhale deeply as if it were the finest fragrance in the world and encourage us to do the same. I could never tell if she was serious or just pulling our legs, but she really seemed to relish the overpowering aroma.

We also did our shopping the Dutch way—that is to say, daily, so that everything was sure to be fresh. It was necessary, anyway, because their tiny refrigerators could not hold a week's worth of groceries, and their freezer compartments were miniscule. We ate out a lot, at any rate, so we could experience the variety of Dutch cultural influences. One evening, we ate at an Indonesian restaurant which offered "rijstafel," a Dutch favorite, which provides an array of dishes heavy on the curry. Most of it was very tasty, but for whatever reason, I could not stand the skewers of beef dipped in peanut butter sauce. I like peanut butter, but not with meat! I got violently ill, and Lida, for some reason, was chillingly unsympathetic. Other than that, the trip was a big success!

One of the big excursions was to Zaandvoort to see the Grand Prix, which, unfortunately, ended in tragedy when a British racer was killed in the course of the race. It was hot on the dunes, and I would have loved a frosty coke, but, alas, it was not meant to be. Pepsi was available, but far from being frosty, it was hot! Of course, in Texas, we like our drinks ice-cold, so that was a shock to my cultural sensibilities. We also took Delia to see Madurodam, a miniature village so detailed, it had a re-creation of Schiphol—the Dutch airport. For Delia, it was magic, seeing the tiny people who populated the little villages. Everywhere we went and everything we saw far surpassed anything I could ever have imagined!

Through the duration of the two week stay, Johanna was the consummate tour guide. Every site we visited was filtered through her historical commentary. We didn't just look at a castle or fortification; we learned who lived there and when, what is was used for, why it was important historically, and how it's maintained. She was so well-versed in the history of her country, she could even point out dents in the building's structure that were actually bullet holes from some battle or other. She insisted that we climb into the towers so that we could get the view and understand how strategically the fortifications had been placed and also for the aesthetic angle—the beautiful vistas afforded by the height. If we were in a museum—and we often were—she knew the artists, their techniques, their time frames, the significance of the different works, the texture, etc., etc. She especially loved the Dutch masters, and her reverence for them rubbed off on me. The Dutch School is still my favorite. Whenever I am in Amsterdam, I head straight for the Rijksmuseum to see my old friends—the Rembrandts, the Vermeers, the Hals and the Averkamps. Johanna had an eye for detail, and she loved pointing out the tiny things in the paintings that made them so lively: the children, the dogs, the fruit on the table, the warmth of the hearth. One painting in particular always got a laugh from her. In the bottom right corner of a very busy Dutch domestic scene, there are two tiny dogs frolicking. Someone just passing through and giving the painting a preemptory glance probably would not notice it, but for Johanna, it was the small things that counted. She was a pretty good artist herself, having given me a copy of a sketch she once did of Wolfgang. When I asked her how she was able to draw such a good likeness, she said that it was "all geometry; the relation of one feature of the face to another, and the perspective."

That first trip ended all too soon. There would never be another one quite like it. The next time Delia and I went, in 1974, she was six years old; her beloved Dutch "Omama" was now in a nursing home and had lost much of her short-term memory. She seemed to be living in the past, once addressing my ex-husband as "Herr Kommandant," as though he were a German soldier. It was sad to see someone who had been so vital, so intelligent, so forceful, reduced to this tiny woman completely lost in the shrouds of time. It was the last time we saw her alive. Tante Lida sold the house and moved to an apartment in Amstelveen, a suburb of Amsterdam, so subsequent trips lost much of their charm for me.

In the meantime, Johanna and I stayed close, frequently collaborating on programs and activities designed to educate Delia and provide her with a cultural background. She was always very generous because she knew that, as a teacher, I did not make enough money to provide a lot of extracurricular activities for her. During the summer, we would share the cost of sending Delia to camp, swimming and tennis lessons, music lessons, including flute and piano, dance lessons, and, later, driving lessons. She was always supportive and very involved in Delia's life. After Wolf died and she retired, she stayed busy with her "projects." She resumed weaving and bought a huge loom which almost filled up her huge back room. This would necessitate her traveling to South America for special yarn, which in turn would inspire her to take Spanish lessons. She always had something interesting going on. For her, learning was a lifelong passion. Politics fascinated her. Travel remained a huge part of her life until she was in her seventies and decided that she needed to stay close to her doctor. Until that point, she had kept a small apartment in a suburb of Driebergen called Bunnik. She typically went every summer and used Bunnik as her headquarters for further adventures to visit old friends in other parts of Europe. As she grew older and more cautious about her health, she curtailed her visits to Europe, which I know was difficult for her. But as many of her friends passed away, she had less motivation to make the long journey.

When Tante Lida got sick, she went into a nursing home. Years before, she had started visiting a facility that was near her apartment to get to know the people there; she often had dinner with the residents. Once she began to have health issues, she felt comfortable moving there, and she deteriorated rather quickly. Having survived breast cancer, she now succumbed to dementia, and it quickly took its toll. It is fortunate that she had the foresight to recognize the symptoms because of her mother's illness and was able to plan ahead for the inevitable. By the fall of 1999, it was clear that she was failing fast, and Delia made the decision to go during Thanksgiving break to visit her for what turned out to be the last time. Johanna had neither the inclination nor the strength to make the trip, so Delia made the journey in what I consider to be a courageous and humanitarian effort. Tante Lida lived her life, resentful to the end, thinking that no one really cared for her. Despite that, she genuinely cared for Delia, and Delia felt that it was her responsibility to show Tante Lida a final act of kindness and love. The visit was difficult for Delia; Tante Lida was dying and a mere vestige of her former, vibrant, imposing self. But Delia went to spend time with her, talking to her, even when Lida didn't seem to comprehend what was going on. She was chatty and charming, letting Tante Lida know that she was loved. It was the last time anyone in the family would see Lida before she died.

That trip had its funny side, too. When I went to the airport to pick Delia up, the strangest-looking people disembarked with her. People with long hair and beards, jeans with chains, denim jackets—people who seemed to have stepped right out of *Easy Rider*. I asked, "What kind of ZZ Top-freak show did you get hooked up with?" She laughed and said, "You won't believe it, but Thanksgiving week is apparently *High Times' Magazine's* annual marijuana convention in Amsterdam. I stayed in a hotel in the Leidesplein, and I met up with an American who told me that he is an editor for *HighTimes,* and that all of the hippies were there for the convention." "But," she continued, "Half of them got pulled off the flight when we landed in Atlanta to go through customs. Apparently customs knew about the convention, too, and they went through EVERYONE'S baggage. It was no random thing; we all got searched, and a lot of those idiots thought they could smuggle some samples back!" I still laugh when I think about my conventional high school-teaching daughter getting off that flight with Captain America!

AFTERWORD

Without a doubt, Johanna was instrumental in enriching my life. She was so lively and fun, keen for adventure. She was a unique individual who did not bite her tongue; she could be refreshingly honest or brutally frank. Although she lived in the United States for over sixty years, she never lost her thick Dutch accent. It was a part of her charm. We bonded over our mutual love of animals. She loved to come to my house and visit with the dogs, cats, and bunnies. They amused her to no end. At one time, she had one of those half-dollar-sized turtles that you buy at a dime store, but when it got too big for the aquarium, she took it to the Dallas Zoo so it could have a better life. When I first met her, she had a fat tabby cat ironically named "Mouse." And I will never forget the afternoon she looked out the window to my back yard and saw a little terrier trying to mount a big Labrador-mixed dog. She screamed with laughter and yelled, "Look! That leetle dog is trying to fock that beeg dog!" Johanna's command of the English language was perfect, and she knew very well the shock value associated with certain American expressions. She also delighted in showing her mischievous side. There was, literally, never a dull moment when Johanna was around. She made it a point to keep abreast of the latest trends; often, she was ahead of the curve. In the late sixties, she was the one to introduce me to composting. No one else that I knew had ever even heard of it. She was passionate about its benefits and keen to enlighten others. And recycling was on her agenda long before "Earth Day" and other environmental measures were initiated. I think she would be very pleased to know how committed people are to conserving the environment now and reversing the damage that has already been done.

Even in death, she is sending me on adventures. My research into her life has provided me with new associates—from Seattle, Washington to Jena, Germany. People who knew her or are interested in her story have contacted me. Through her, I have forged bonds with several people who, like me, are eager to preserve the past and share the stories of their loved ones.

Since I embarked on this journey, I have often wondered why she chose me to be the "keeper of the flame" when she had other relatives to whom she could have entrusted her story. After all, I am the ex-daughter-in-law, although she always introduced me to people in the present tense. I feel blessed that she chose me. She was a remarkable woman who deserves recognition for a life well-lived and a job well-done. Her work in World War II is nothing short of heroic. But it didn't end there; she spent her life caring for others. She cared for Wolf in his final days at home. It was his fervent desire not to die in a sterile hospital environment, and she made sure that he was given the best possible care in the comforts of his home at a time that hospice care did not exist.

At his funeral, attended only by family and a few close friends, she honored his request to have no formal service; instead, she played his favorite piece from the "Hunt Quartet," the same music that Ton Akkerman whistled to summon Wolfgang from his hiding place in the attic when Johanna had come to visit so many years before.

In her final act of kindness and concern for mankind, like her cousin Jan, Johanna willed her body to science so that she continued to be a tool for education even in death.

Well, Johanna, this is it. I hope that I have done justice to your story. You gave me the seeds of the story so to speak, and it kept growing. I hope you are pleased with the outcome. Thank you for launching me on this adventure. It has been a true learning experience beyond anything I could have imagined. Delia reminded me that your favorite expression was, "Well, folks, that's the way the cookie crumbles." I believe that philosophy is what sustained you through some of the most harrowing events in the history of mankind and enabled you to maintain such a positive outlook. No matter how bleak a situation might have been, you forged ahead, determined to make the best of everything. I will never forget the sight of you, dancing with Delia with such abandon, with such a light heart and with such a carefree spirit. Your *joie de vivre*, despite everything you experienced and witnessed, is what made you such a joy and such a treasure. I am blessed to have known you and cherish the memory of the time we spent together. Tot ziens!

TRIBUTES TO JOHANNA

After my article about Johanna was published in the *Dallas Morning News*, I received several emails from people who were touched by the story. To this day, I occasionally receive emails from people who, in the course of their research about the Holocaust, or Zeiss-Eicon, or the Herschowitsch family, run across the article and are moved to comment.

December 6, 2009
Leonard Comess, M.D.:
"I read your beautiful tribute to Johanna this morning. I had the privilege of serving as her doctor for many years. I had no idea that she behaved so heroically during the Nazi Occupation. As a Jew, I am especially moved by her story and wish that I had known so I could have thanked her in person. Thank you for your article."

Mitta Angel:
"I just read your wonderful tribute to your mother-in-law, Johanna Herschkowitsch. I joined the Dallas Symphony in 1965 and knew her well. She and Wolfgang were wonderful people with whom I played chamber music on several occasions. Over the years, since her retirement, I've sadly lost touch, but remember her fondly. She was a wonderful woman and it's lovely to know that you appreciated her so much."

December 14, 2009
Elliott Dlin, Executive Director, Dallas Holocaust Museum/Center for Education and Tolerance:
"I read your article of December 6, 2009 in the *Dallas Morning News* with interest. Your

mother-in-law's story sounds very interesting and I was intrigued by your reference to a videotape of at least part of her testimony.

We have an archival collection of some 250 testimonies of Holocaust survivors, helpers and protectors, as well as liberators and we would be most interested to add a copy of Johanna Herschkowitsch's story.

Would you be willing to allow us to copy the tape? Did your mother-in-law have any photographs or documents that we might also duplicate and that would provide a broader understanding of her life and actions?

Since you are a high school teacher, I should also inquire whether you are familiar with our museum, our tours for students, our workshops for teachers, and the curricula that we offer?

I look forward to hearing from you. Warmest holiday greetings to you and yours."

December 15, 2009
Camille W:
"Thank you for the article about your mother-in-law. I find it amazing what brave things were done during WWII on both the military and civilian side. I cannot imagine living with the level of fear your mother-in-law and her friends lived with, especially when defying Nazi orders. It is amazing. To be reunited with her musician friend, to marry him and spend years playing in the Dallas Symphony - what an example of the triumph of human bravery and caring."

Shelley and Simma Weiss:
"Thank you for your article in the *Dallas Morning News*, 'A real heroine of her time.' It is a wonderful tribute to your mother-in-law and an inspiration to your readers. May we never again

know such dark times. We extend our condolences to you, and pray that her memory will always be such a blessing. Thanks again for publishing on such a special and heroic lady."

December 21, 2009
Arthur Ephross:
"I just received a copy of your article about my old friends Wolfgang and Johanna who were my colleagues when I was a member of the DSO - of course some time back. In all the time I knew them I never heard this story and it is very emotional to read it. Thank you for bringing it to the attention of the world."

April 13, 2012
Dr. Peter Crane, Seattle:
"Dear Cynthia Herschkowitsch, I liked very much the article you wrote about your late mother-in-law. I wish I had met her. I talked with her on the phone a few years ago, and thought that I should make a trip to Texas to see her. I thought you would like to know that there is a historian in Germany interested in knowing more about the Herschkowitsch family. Based on your article, I did Google and Google Books searches on Johanna's father, W. Van Dam, and I see that there is a great deal written by and about him. If you search his name, along with 'butter,' 'pasteurization,' or 'cheese,' you will get more sites than you will know what to do with. I am no blood relative of the Herschkowitsch family; Jela Herschkowitsch was the sister-in-law of my grandmother."

Cynthia Herschkowitsch

Cynthia Herschkowitsch, a resident of Carrollton, Texas, taught English and German in Dallas, Texas, for 39 years. In 1987-88, she was named Dallas Independent School District's Teacher of the Year. During her career, she coached Academic Decathlon, served as coordinator for graduation activities, and coordinated the University Interscholastic League academic events. For over 20 years, she hosted a Christmas party for needy children at the school with the help of her students and was twice named Fox 4's "Hometown Hero" by news anchor Clarice Tinsley for her charitable work. She is a regular contributor to the Neighborhood Voices column of the *Dallas Morning News* and remains active in education and community activities. She has also been an animal rescuer for 30 years, working closely with the SPCA of Texas in Dallas, Operation Kindness, and Stray Dog, Inc. Her favorite pastimes are traveling, reading, and spending time with family, friends and pets, especially her little dog, J.B. She especially enjoys collaborating with her daughter Delia and her former students on special events.

Proof

Made in the USA
Charleston, SC
08 May 2015